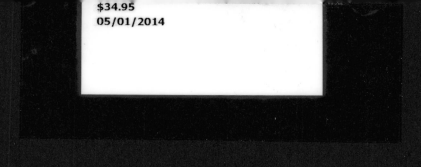

A HOME IN PROVENCE

INTERIORS · GARDENS · INSPIRATION

Text by Noëlle Duck · Photography by Christian Sarramon

Flammarion

CONTENTS

INTRODUCTION
HOUSES IN THE SUN

A traveler will always know when he has reached Provence, as soon as the first stone houses come into view, their gently sloping roofs covered in Roman tiles in muted colors. Somewhere near Montélimar, the gateway to the Land of the Mistral, the walls begin to be built of bare, golden stones piled roughly on top of each other, giving houses of the Drôme the look of sheepfolds. Farther to the south, there are the *bastides*, elegant farmhouses glimpsed between the cool greenery of the trees that huddle around them. The bright or pastel colors of the stuccoed frontages of village houses stand out amid the trees lining the streets, looking like a Neapolitan ice cream with their raspberry, peach, and green almond hues. Before reaching the Camargue, whose little houses look like upturned boats covered with thatched roofs, the visitor will notice the stone country houses with pale lavender or deep olive shutters; these dot the landscape around Aix-en-Provence, between the Alpilles and the Luberon. A land of sun, wind, and heat, southern France is also a land of stone, ocher, and terra-cotta.

THE HOUSE

BASTIDES, MAS, CABANONS...

The Provençal home is in perfect harmony with its surroundings.
It is south facing, not to welcome the sun but to turn its back
on the Mistral, the bitter north wind that blows in furious gusts.

An avenue of plane trees leads to the cool mansion, concealing its secrets. If the house stands by the sea, date palms, whose heavy bunches of orange fruits will never ripen, may form a stiff, evergreen colonnade on the steep hillside. Or there may be young pine trees, almost certainly planted by an outsider, because the local people dislike this tree that bursts into flame so readily, flinging out burning branches that can set light to anything within miles. In the Camargue, however, in the arid plain of La Crau where forest fires are an impossibility, a clump of umbrella pines offering shade to a solitary *mas* is revered like a sacred grove.

Provençal houses are always surrounded by trees, just as once they always had a well. Even the humblest of stone huts, in the middle of nowhere, will be marked by the green splash of a plane, mulberry, or linden tree, rising above the grapevines to provide the residents with a little shade at the hottest time of day. The sign of human habitation in Provence is always a patch of greenery: sometimes a tall cane or cypress hedge protecting fields of melons or eggplant; sometimes a massive, untidy clump of wild mimosa. Most important of all are the cypress trees, the traditional trees of welcome, planted by the entrance, usually in pairs.

BASTIDES

From the fifteenth century onward a *bastide* has always referred to a substantial property in the country. Such properties were inhabited by nobles, by the wealthiest families of Aix-en-Provence and Marseilles, by landowners and winery proprietors. The landscape around Aix and the vineyards of the Var district contain many such impressive residences, which bear a passing resemblance to Palladian villas, with their square shape, four-sided roofs, stone

PAGE 12:
A few craftsmen have maintained the tradition of the wooden bead curtain, a unique and understated screen between the cool shade of the corridor and the bright sunlight outside.

FACING PAGE:
In the hands of Édith Mezard, the Château d'Ange at Groult in the Luberon bears fine witness to the art of living in Provence.

dados, and simple, elegant forms. Some *bastides* are "follies," miniature châteaux set in gardens in which fountains play. These were clearly built as country retreats. Others are just two-story dwellings, but all have tall windows with small windowpanes that are rigorously symmetrical, and identical in shape on the first and second floors. The windows are designed to let in plenty of air in the summer. A *bastide* may have a third story, used as an attic or as servants' sleeping quarters. The space is lit by a row of small square or circular windows framed by stone cladding or, more rarely, by a brick surround.

The front door is often imposing, and is positioned symmetrically in the center of the façade. Three steps may lead up to it. The doorway is reinforced with stone slabs, topped by two cornerstones to accentuate the keystone. These door frames can still be found through dealers in architectural features, some removed from buildings that are little more than stone huts.

The *bastides* owned by middle-class families tend to be plainer and less pretentious than those owned by nobility, and remain largely unchanged. The beautifully balanced proportion of the façade does not overpower the outbuildings, which have been added to compensate for the lack of cellars.

The term *bastide* has been wrongly applied to smaller, dilapidated stone buildings, which are properly known as *bastidons*. These single-story dwellings are located near villages, often by the roadside. Some have been converted into antiques stores, but because of their close proximity and easy access to the villages, they also make delightful guesthouses.

HÔTELS PARTICULIERS

The *hôtels particuliers* of the well-to-do were intended to show the wealth and good taste of the owner, and they do not always look typically Provençal. They were often owned by senior judges, powerful civil servants, and even noblemen attending the French court at Versailles. The architecture of these seventeenth- and eighteenth-century houses was based on Parisian styles, but adapted to the Provençal setting and climate. They were decorated by local and regional artists, craftsmen and sculptors, ironsmiths, and cabinetmakers, whose originality gave them a reputation that stretched as far as Paris.

PAGE 16:
This *mas* in Bonnieux has been rendered using a coating lightly tinted with ocher, a color that harmonizes well with the pastel blue of its shutters.

PAGE 17:
The carved stone cornice underlines the classic style of the front door of this village house.

FACING PAGE:
The Château de Barbentane in the Alpilles is considered the Versailles of Provence.

PAGES 20 & 21:
Mascarons, door knockers, and sculpted friezes have embellished fountains and doors since the Renaissance, while the interior façades of *hôtels particuliers* in Nice and Aix-en-Provence bear an obvious resemblance.

FACING PAGE:
This interior courtyard is brightened up with a red ocher rendering.

RIGHT:
The strict symmetry of this Louis XIV façade is softened by the delicate wrought-ironwork of the balcony.

PAGES 24–25:
A wide path bordered by a double row of box leads to the Château de Sauvan, nicknamed the "Petit Trianon de Provence."

MAS ARE DELIGHTFUL, UNOSTENTATIOUS DWELLINGS, THEIR STONE FAÇADES COVERED WITH CRUMBLING, FADED, BUT AUTHENTIC PLASTERWORK.

The door is flanked by columns, and male and female figures seem to be supporting the central balcony. This balcony is larger than the rest, and is reminiscent of the loggias of Venetian palazzos, designed to enable people to watch the world go by, and to be used as an extension to the brilliantly lit reception room behind. The tall French windows lead onto small, narrow balconies, whose wrought-iron balustrades have a light and fragile appearance so as not to spoil the style of the façade. The mansions in the old quarter of Aix-en-Provence, and those that line the main street, the Cours Mirabeau, are greatly admired by summer visitors, who gaze at the wrought-ironwork that was the pride of local craftsmen. The tall French windows of the *hôtels particuliers* belonging to the nobility, like those of the most elegant *bastides*, are shutterless on the outside, but have solid wooden shutters inside to protect the privacy of the inhabitants.

MAS AND MAZETS

These are less ostentatious but nevertheless delightful dwellings. The stone façade is covered with crumbling, faded, but authentic plasterwork, through which the original stonework is visible in places, prompting the question: should all the plaster be removed, exposing the bare stonework, or should it be repaired, restored, and painted ocher? The woodwork, doors, and shutters are painted in a contrasting color, the window frames usually being coated in white gloss paint. Houses that have been too heavily restored and have that "good-as-new" look should be shunned: they represent the opposite of the lived-in look that is typically Provençal. Restoration should be discreet and modest, to blend in with the stone-and-brick constructions that are the legacy of the Roman occupation; it was Roman architects who introduced these styles.

A *mas* is a farmhouse, or some sort of farming concern. In Provence, the *mas* owner grows herbs, spring vegetables or tomatoes, peppers, eggplant, and melons, and also tends small orchards of peach, apricot, apple, and pear trees. In the Camargue, the *mas* is the home of the owner of the *manade*, the ranch on which fighting bulls are reared.

FACING PAGE:
A climbing vine or wisteria provides shade in summer while still allowing the sun to warm the terrace in winter.

PAGES 28–29:
The openings of the buildings of this former farmhouse near Saint-Rémy have been framed with a whitewash rendering.

LEFT:
A simple awning made from *canisse* (Provence cane screening)—a multipurpose material in Provence—protects the terrace here.

FACING PAGE:
Sheltered from the world behind such lovely shutters, one cannot help but feel contented.

A CABANON IS A MINIATURE HOUSE, DESIGNED AS A PLACE WHERE FARMWORKERS, TOILING IN THE FIELDS, COULD REST AT THE HOTTEST TIMES OF DAY.

When a *mas* is large it often has a number of outbuildings, which surround the main building in a horseshoe shape. This produces an assortment of different roof heights.

In the Camargue the living rooms are on the ground floor and the bedrooms on the floor above. In the districts of Haut-Var and Alpes-de-Haute-Provence the ground floor is low-ceilinged. It may be used for storage; again, there are no cellars, because it is impossible to dig them out of the rocky terrain. The occupants live on the upper floor, or rather on a mezzanine, accessible via an outside staircase, the main entrance being protected by a small stoop. This type of building offers many architectural possibilities, and a pleasant life on a single floor, above ground level. The windows are plain with small panes, or in two sections when they are more modern, and are sometimes protected by solid shutters.

A *mazet* is a little *mas*; like most diminutives, it is also used as a term of endearment. This single-story farm building sometimes has storage for farm machinery. It comes with a small plot of land and may have been built for a young farming couple, or given to a tenant-farmer. In the Camargue the word describes a low, whitewashed building with a thatched roof, built with its back to the Mistral. These were once occupied by watchmen.

CABANONS AND BORIES

A *cabanon* is a miniature house, designed as a place where farmworkers, toiling in the fields, could rest at the hottest times of day. With its well-balanced proportions, it can be converted into a delightful vacation retreat. It is almost always built of exposed stonework with a two-sided, pitched, slightly overhanging roof with no eaves. The façade has no embellishment other than the arched door frame, made of stone blocks, which may date from the eighteenth or nineteenth century. If there are any windows at all, they are tiny.

There are also *cabanons* that were originally built as weekend homes for urban families of modest means, mainly from Marseilles or Toulon. They were often used as an escape from the stifling heat of the city, or as beach chalets; they could be used to house a few chairs and a table, deck chairs, and a tripod to hold a soup pot in which to cook a bouillabaisse. That is the origin of the *cabanons* along the *calanques* (inlets) at Sormiou, between Marseilles and

FACING PAGE:
Cabanons are still used to store tools and other supplies. Many of those that have a well and a handsome tree beside them have become country homes for city dwellers.

FACING PAGE:
Isolated in the middle of an olive grove, the *cabanon* is a place of solitude, a romantic retreat in the heart of Provence.

RIGHT:
Bories have never served as human dwellings, as is evident from the very low entrance, but rather are used as places for storage and as shelter for sheep during storms.

FISHERMEN'S HOUSES WERE BUILT AT THE WATERSIDE, FACING THE QUAY, HUDDLED TOGETHER IN A ROW. ALTHOUGH PAINTED IN CONTRASTING COLORS, THEIR TWO-STORY FAÇADES ARE IDENTICAL, AND THEY MAKE AN ATTRACTIVE TERRACE OF HOUSES.

Cassis, and those on the Giens peninsula. They were always shaded by pine trees for siestas, and situated near water so that the children could play.

Bories are found deep in the Luberon. They are round huts of dry stonework, like the houses in the Gordes region. There is nothing typically Provençal about their architecture and materials: they are even found in the Vendée. They were mere toolsheds, and places for sheep to shelter during a storm, as can be seen by the very low opening. They were probably never used for living in. They are a quaint vestige of how Provençal country folk lived, but could not possibly be converted into a home.

OLD VILLAGE OR TOWN HOUSES

The largest of the old village or town houses were often occupied by an order of nuns, by prominent people, or by leading families. Sometimes they were the home of wealthy craftsmen or merchants, who lived over the store. They are stone built, but they are plastered so that only the cornerstones are exposed. They are often tall, to capture as much as possible of the dim light of the narrow streets. Inland the shutters are solid, but toward the sea they are louvered, and in the Nice region they take the form of jalousies—shutters that have adjustable louvers to let in light and air while keeping out rain or sun. In Nice and along the Ligurian Coast they may also take the form of partisols. These are louvered shutters made in two parts, so that the upper part can be opened to allow cool air to circulate while the bottom part remains closed.

The fishermen's houses at Martigues or on the canal de Beaucaire at Tarascon have largely become artists' colonies. They were built at the waterside, facing the quay, huddled together in a row. Although painted in contrasting colors, their two-story façades are identical, and they make an attractive terrace of houses. The rooms occupied by day are on the ground floor, so that when the windows are open the inhabitants can chat to passers-by. Ideally, fishing boats belonging to the owners could be moored right in front of the house, as they are in Port Grimaud.

To restore the original style and character to a Provençal house, it is a good idea to frequent antique and junk stores, and yards dealing in recycled

FACING PAGE:
At Saint-Tropez, the tall, narrow façades of houses facing the harbor are illuminated by the setting sun.

PAGES 38 & 39:
Shutters of every size—louvered or solid—shelter every opening and provide protection from the heat and wind.

IT IS STONE THAT KEEPS THE HOUSE UPRIGHT AND GIVES IT ITS IMPOSING FAÇADE—AS PALE AS ARLESIAN GIRLS, WHO ARE CAREFUL NEVER TO EXPOSE THEMSELVES TO THE SUN.

architectural materials—including roof tiles. Mixing pigments in large quantities to get just the right shade for the plaster is a highly skilled job, as is removing dilapidated plaster, without damaging the stones underneath, to create an exposed stone frontage. However, it is possible to take courses where you can learn all aspects of restoring and remodeling a house; these are run by experts in traditional techniques who are qualified to guide the amateur and thus prevent any serious errors.

WALLS

Stone is used for all types of houses because the local limestone, which stretches from the sea to the foothills of the Alps, is a readily available raw material. The stone was quarried and the quarries were free, meaning that—provided they extracted it themselves—anyone who needed stone could simply take it. When peasants cleared the stones that littered their fields, they would store them for future construction use. The quarry on the route des Crêtes at Bormes-les-Mimosas, a lovely hilltop village in Var Maritime used to provide schist, a blood-red sandstone sprinkled with gold that used to be cut in the form of ingots. On the Estérel coast at Bandol, it was used for building houses that blended seamlessly into the landscape. It is a perfect match, and is also used for garden walls. Bormes stone was the ideal material for some of the registered historic buildings beside the sea, where houses were allowed to have only one floor: the color made them almost invisible. Along the banks of the Durance, and in the foothills of the Alpilles where the River Rhône once ran, there is a wonderful deposit of smooth pebbles that are perfect for the façades and walls of dry-stone enclosures, especially when they are tinted red by silica deposits, as in the Châteauneuf-du-Pape district. The quarries at Cassis, the most recent to have closed, provided splendid white stone, as fine as marble, and blocks from which circular kitchen sinks (*piles*) were hollowed out.

Until the 1980s, old houses were often covered with a fresh coat of plaster. Some of these buildings were very old, with lovely proportions, high ceilings, and stone frontages covered with smooth plasterwork that dated from the late nineteenth century. They were modernized by being coated with pinkish-beige plaster, curiously known as *rose de brignoles*, thrown on with a trowel, or deliberately roughened to give a "rustic" look. The historic districts of the

FACING PAGE:
This contemporary house near Gordes respects the local dry-stone construction methods—obligatory in this registered historic area!

PAGES 42–43:
An array of colorful façades and shutters along one of the two canals at Martigues, the "Venice of Provence." It is said that the fishermen painted their houses with paint left over from sprucing up their boats.

LEFT:
Amble around the villages, with their narrow streets that the sun struggles to penetrate, to discover old houses like these.

FACING PAGE:
The advantage and charm of rendering tinted with ocher pigments—as here at Roussillon—is that it never looks new and does not fade in the sun.

IT CAN BE HOPED THAT THE PROVENÇAL HOUSE,
WHOSE UNIQUE STYLE HAS BEEN SHAPED BY HISTORY
AND THE CONTINGENCIES OF THE CLIMATE,
HAS FINALLY BEEN RESCUED FROM PASTICHE
AND DISFIGURATION.

cities of Provence lost all their style, charm, and authenticity. Places such as Cotignac, standing against its hill; Saint-Paul-de-Vence with its little squares with their fountains; the bright red façades of old Nice; the Cours Mirabeau in Aix-en-Provence; the quays of Martigues; the "rusty houses" of which Charles Trenet sang—all these were seen as museum pieces. Fortunately, they have served as examples. In Port Grimaud, the architect François Spoerry, inspired by the houses of Burano, the lace-makers' island in the Venice lagoon, restored the colors. The bell tower at Saint-Tropez, whose soft ocher hues are identical to the original shades, has become the archetype for the color scheme of the South of France. It can be hoped that the Provençal house, whose unique style has been shaped by history and the contingencies of the climate, has finally been rescued from pastiche and disfiguration.

Openings naturally depend on the location of the house and the style of its façade. But they have one thing in common: they are always larger when south facing, because in this direction they are facing away from the Mistral. They can also welcome in the penetrating light from the winter sun, which is very low on the horizon at that time of year.

Bastides typically have tall French windows with small panes. *Mas* and other types of country house have plain casement windows with two panes; this same design can be used to make French windows in traditionally built villas. Wherever necessary, and so that the windows can be kept open, especially during the summer heat, there is a second frame—between the window and the shutters—where fly screens can be fitted. A little brass window-catch operates the rod by which the fly screen is attached to the main frame.

Everywhere—in the town and country alike, but never in the homes of dignitaries and noblemen—the front door was protected by beaded curtains that served a multiplicity of purposes. They let air enter while leaving the flies outside, made it possible to leave the front door open while maintaining a sense of privacy, brought some shade to a south-facing corridor, and made it possible to see anyone coming to the door without being seen. The bead curtain was rather inconvenient, though, and nearly became obsolete, but was saved by a few purist artisans. To preserve it in spirit, a curtain of light material—cheesecloth or muslin, for example—can be used to cover the doorway.

FACING PAGE:
Leading to an interior courtyard, this doorway in an ocher-rendered façade is framed with white stone.

PAGES 48–49:
The houses and *bories* of the hilltop village of Gordes, in the Vaucluse, are built from dry stone, that is without using mortar.

ROOFS ALWAYS SLOPE GENTLY. AS THERE IS LITTLE
RAINFALL IN PROVENCE, THE RAIN DOES NOT NEED
TO DRAIN OFF RAPIDLY. MOREOVER, THE ROOF NEEDS
TO PRESENT THE LEAST POSSIBLE WIND RESISTANCE.

It will move at the slightest breath of air, but will preserve the privacy of the interior and will be a delightful and practical feature.

ROOFS AND GÉNOISES

Mas, *bastidons*, and the farmhouses of some of the more prosperous vineyards have two-sided roofs that overlap the frontages. Under the gables, there is a circular window to illuminate the attic, and often a horizontal pantile or even a little molded cornice.

Detached houses in the countryside all conform to strict rules. The front entrance must be south facing, letting in plenty of sunshine and light, which is filtered by the trees in summer. Above all, it must be sheltered from the wind. The north-facing frontage has much smaller openings and the gables are blind because the Mistral and Tramontane blow from the north and west respectively, and the rain comes from the east.

Village houses usually have one or two rooms per floor and are three or four stories high. They are narrow, and generally terraced or in rows. The roof is a pitched lean-to, without a *génoise* (see page 56), but with a deep overhang to protect the frontage, or a little terrace used for drying laundry or for growing fruits and vegetables.

The houses are of different heights and, viewed from above, the roofs present an ancient patchwork, the lines broken by the various angles and directions of roof pitch, sometimes spiraling around a church or château. There is nothing to spoil the monochrome of drystone walls and terra-cotta, so typical of the part of Drôme that is in Provence, and of the *départements* of Alpes-de-Haute-Provence and the numerous hilltop villages such as La Cadière-d'Azur, Lacoste, Le Castellet, or Forcalqueiret.

The Roman tile is a semi-cylinder of terra-cotta, shaped by women on their thighs, whose color depends upon the type of local clay used to make it. The tiles are laid in overlapping rows to ensure that they remain waterproof, alternating with upturned or flat tiles, the latter being fixed to the roofbeams and called the "run-off" tiles. Roman-tiled roofs need to be consolidated and

FACING PAGE:
A view over the rooftops of Ménerbes, in the heart of the Luberon. The tall house with pale blue shutters was once the home of the painter Nicolas de Staël.

LEFT:
In the past, these concave or Roman tiles were made from local clay of varying tones. Mossy, marked, and patinated, they have the charm of old ceramics.

PAGES 54 & 55:
Génoises are often present below the roof overhang to prevent rainwater running onto the walls.

ventilated so that the clay does not snap at extremes of temperature, so they ought to be insulated from the roof beams. The traditional technique for achieving this is called "Arlesian roofing," and involves filling the spaces beneath the covering tiles with Provence cane (which is neither bamboo nor reed, but the stalks of cereals). The air can circulate lengthwise between the canes, which, if well aerated, will not rot. This roofing technique, which builders have stopped using now, has been revived by the Monuments Historiques organization for the restoration of ancient buildings, especially in Arles and Marseilles. As an excellent contemporary solution using ancient know-how—which was perfectly adapted for use on channel tiles—it deserves to be reinstated for use in private homes, since the raw material is abundant and inexpensive.

Génoises are single, double, triple, or even quadruple rows of upturned Roman tiles that are fixed to walls below the roofline, an elegant feature that also helps to deflect rain from the walls. Gables do not have *génoises* beneath them, though the roof will often overhang by several rows of tiles at the gable ends. There are two types of *génoise*, hollow or filled, depending on whether the tiles rest on mortar or on *malons*, known as *maloun* in Provençal. *Malons* are squares of enameled tile. Rectangular terra-cotta tiles are interspersed lengthwise between the rows of *génoises*, or even Roman tiles, a souvenir of the 1950s fashion that found them everywhere on balconies, terraces, and garden walls.

Despite the name, which means Genoese, *génoises* are rare on houses in Nice, a city that was once under Italian rule. Here the *genoises* are replaced by deep overhangs of tiles attached to semi-circular rafters, beneath which the walls are decorated with Italianate frescoes. *Hôtels particuliers* in Aix-en-Provence and Arles, *bastides*, certain old *mas*, and the large square nineteenth-century village houses built by prosperous local dignitaries are often embellished with plaster or stone cornices.

FACING PAGE:
The ground floor of some *bastides*, as in Palladian villas, is raised above the storehouses, forming a wide terrace.

THE INTERIORS

LIVING IN THE HOUSE

Outdoors, beyond the shady garden, the burning sun, the gusting Mistral, and the utter dryness of summer prevail. The half-closed shutters and thin muslin curtain screening the open front door block out the heat. Once over the threshold, the cool, pale ocher walls, terra-cotta tiled floors, and stone stairs combine to help one gradually cool down from the stifling heat.

The single entrance of the south-facing Provençal house leads directly either into the main living room or, if it has more than one story, into a tiny hallway from which the staircase leads. This room may open into the reception room, kitchen, or even a study. It is often neutral, or at least muted in relation to the decoration that can be glimpsed through the doorways. It may be very elegant, as at the Château de Barbentane, where it sets the opulent tone for the whole interior.

After that, the rooms are arranged in whatever order is most natural. The kitchen, scullery, and its *cafoucho* (a pantry or deep storage space) stands on one side—it sometimes has a small door leading to the outside—and bedrooms on the other. In his book *Les Maisons provençales*, Jean-Luc Massot, an architect from Aix-en-Provence who specializes in the restoration of the local houses, writes: "There is no leeway, no superfluous space, everything seems to merge into a single unit, both on the horizontal plane—the plan—and on the vertical plane—the elevations.... Each of the spaces works as part of the whole. One could not remove any of them without damaging the whole: this is the proof of completeness and maturity."

Although *bastides* have had a separate dining room since the eighteenth century, *mas* and village houses have a large drawing room and a room that serves as a kitchen-cum-dining room. This arrangement is a traditional one, but it is also very convenient and has been happily retained by many new owners. On the upper floor, the best bedrooms are always those that are south facing.

LEFT:
Craftsmen in wrought iron have been creating handrails like this since the seventeenth century, and continue to do so in Provence.

FACING PAGE:
The walls of the Hôtel d'Olivary—one of the finest *hôtels particuliers* in Aix-en-Provence, which can be visited by appointment—are covered with Venetian velvet flocked wallpaper.

PAGES 64 & 65:
The Château de Barbentane displays several features typical of the decorative style of the eighteenth century: ornamental molded plasterwork, including bouquets of flowers; an apple set on the scrolls of a curved chair back; and the splendid flight of wrought-iron handrails beneath an Italianate cupola.

CEILINGS

Ceilings are finished with cornices and friezes; they often have exposed beams and are sometimes brightly colored. However, they may be white, to give a more classic, natural light to a room, allowing the furnishings and fabrics to contribute brilliance. In the entrance to a house with several stories, whether a town house or a *bastide*, all attention is on the staircase, which winds its red-tiled steps around its light, ethereal wrought iron handrail and balustrading. In such a house, the ceilings and walls of the entrance hall—which is often a room of modest proportions since it is wasted space—are painted in the same pale ocher, or whitewashed for purity, in order to highlight the flooring of terra-cotta or marble and the staircase. In the living rooms the ceilings are finished with cornices or, if the walls were designed to be papered, with curved edging. The cornices may be of plain plaster or wooden moldings, and form the junction between the walls and the ceilings. If painted in strong colors, they add focus to a room and make the ceilings look higher. Below these moldings there are sometimes painted landscapes or frescoes, the equivalent of the painted canvases and scenic wallpaper that decorate the *hôtels particuliers*. In the nineteenth century, wealthy farmers would often ask a local artist or journeyman painter to decorate their homes in this way.

The salon or parlor is the room for special occasions and family gatherings. In some houses, the ceilings are beautifully decorated in plasterwork; in others, where the beams are close together, they are painted with patterns. Local artists adapted the ornate style of Versailles, which was too elaborate for Provence, by using darker colors and Italianate garlands and swags.

It is not unusual to find ceilings whose painted beams are in good condition. A wonderful effect can be achieved by harmonizing the colors of the ceiling with those of the walls: white for the plasterwork, olive green or burnt sienna for the beams, all in matte paint. Ceilings with several rows of beams, known as plastered beams, have plaster molding that links them crosswise; these are called *gypseries*. Coffered ceilings have two rows of beams at right angles to each other, the rectangular spaces in between being called coffers.

The bedrooms, which are really just used for taking a siesta or for sleeping in at night, are much less elaborately decorated than the reception rooms. Here, the ceiling is often whitewashed, plastered, or painted in white, to induce a peaceful sleep.

PAGE 66:
A stoneware vinegar maker—an essential item in the Provençal kitchen—sits next to the beautiful chimney breast, which is enhanced by a collection of old jugs.

PAGE 67:
Avoiding pastiche, the Bastide de Marie at Ménerbes assembles a joyful mixture of objects to charming effect.

FACING PAGE:
The plaster-and-wood ceilings of farmhouses are known as à *caisses*.

THE FIREPLACE IS AN IMPORTANT ELEMENT OF THE INTERIOR, WHETHER IT IS MADE OF STONE, WOOD, OR MARBLE.

PAGE 70:
Renaissance caryatids flank
the chimney breast beneath
a ceiling of painted beams at
the Château de Lourmarin.

PAGE 71:
Another example of the
so-called à caisses ceiling of
wood and plaster.

FACING PAGE:
The fireplace is an essential
part of everyday life, used
for grilling and roasting
food. Stewpots simmer over
the embers on the adjoining
potager, or hearth.

FIREPLACES

A Provençal house would always have a large fireplace in the living room, dining room, or kitchen; besides providing warmth and an attractive focal point, it was important for cooking. The fireplace was used for spit roasting, the spit being attached to large andirons and turned mechanically. Its high hearth meant it could also be used for broiling meat and fish.

Kitchen ranges were built into the stonework, but these have almost completely disappeared; they take up too much space and are no longer useful in the way they were originally. There were two ranges, one with a grate in the center in which the fire was built. An iron tripod was placed over the fire and a cauldron set to cook on it. Embers were removed with tongs to heat the hob. The hob itself was set into an adjacent alcove, and tiled with earthenware tiles. It held a stewpot in which a beef stew (daube) or civet of hare could slowly simmer until it was rich and smooth, while in the oven beneath a tian of vegetables would be baked. Shallow stone or marble circular sinks known as piles were always placed near the kitchen fireplace for convenience.

The châteaux and mansions had fireplaces of marble in various colors, including Turquin blue marble, blue-gray Carrara marble, and a reddish-brown marble streaked with a yellow cement and known as brèche du Tholonet or brèche d'Alep, which was extracted from the Saint-Antonin or Sainte-Victoire quarries. There was also pink marble from Brignoles, red marble from Viterolles; gray Cévenol and marbled stone from Tavel, brocatelle from the Jura and marble from Languedoc. The inventory of the firm of Mazzetty, in Avignon, shows that it was one of the local specialists in this type of marble work, which was used exclusively for mantelpieces and the tops of furniture. The Hôtel de La Mirande in Avignon is a mansion that became a hotel in the 1990s. When restored to its eighteenth-century splendor, it was found to contain a fireplace made principally of Turquin blue marble, with inlaid patterns in red Spanish marble and yellow marble. The hearth is lined with small glazed earthenware tiles from Avignon.

Bedroom fireplaces were generally of plain white or even artificial marble. After the major structural work on a house had been completed, and the plasterers had finished their work, artists of all kinds would arrive: general house painters; specialists in trompe l'oeil, to create wood and marble effects;

FACING PAGE:
The highly architectural fireplace, with its two tiers of white stone, is the main feature of this living room in a house at Bonnieux.

RIGHT:
The bread oven at the Château d'Ansouis, and its fine rounded stone hearth.

PAGES 76–77:
The kitchen in a former barn in the countryside around Grasse, restored by Dirk Bogarde, has been transformed into a living room.

artists who painted on canvas; those who produced patina on furniture; and other craftsmen to add stucco and marble, mirrors and gilding. Some of the small, marble, geometric-shaped fireplaces that were installed in the nineteenth-century, lacking grace and style, have been replaced by wooden fireplaces, the finest ones in well-polished walnut whose patina is evidence of its age.

The best fireplaces are as beautifully carved as wooden furniture. The fronts are curved and sinuous, decorated with a raised, stylized Arles cockleshell, as well as with leaves, fruits, and flowers. From the mid-eighteenth century, fire-places were flat-fronted and fluted. In both cases, they echoed the designs of the furniture. Such fireplaces are collectors' items, highly sought after from specialist dealers. Dealers also sell firedogs, andirons, and hearth backplates in decorative cast iron, sometimes bearing a coat of arms.

It is still possible to find Cassis-stone fireplaces, but they are rarer than marble ones. In the *bastides* or homes of wealthy farmers they were often very large. There are examples at the Mas Calendal at Cassis, and in the home of the poet Frédéric Mistral at Maillane, now a museum. The mantel was tall, rounded or tri-angular, and plastered. Eighteenth-century examples are more heavily worked in dressed stone, with bowed uprights. Sometimes there is a decorative motif in the center of the mantelshelf, often a stylized cockleshell; the overmantel may be decorated with flowers or a Beaucaire mirror in a gilt wood frame.

STAIRCASES

The staircases of Provence—whether of white stonework wound around an elegant balustrade of eighteenth-century wrought iron, or of straight rows of ceramic tiles edged with a nose of polished oak—contribute much to the charm of the interior.

In the *bastides* around Aix-en-Provence and the homes of the wealthy, the staircase was wide, often with half-landings, and edged with high balustrad-ing, with a wrought-iron frieze replacing banisters. The string, to which the balustrading is fixed, was often cut from a single piece of oak; in less well-to-do houses, it was of cement. The balustrading consisted of square sections of

FACING PAGE:
The monastic simplicity of the exposed stone and modern staircase is tempered here by a pretty eighteenth-century painted-wood writing desk.

wrought iron, plain or worked, or of elegant patterns that echoed those of the balconies. Wrought-ironwork has always been a craft appreciated in Provence; the skills involved have been transmitted across generations of families, some of whom have become widely known.

The beauty of a staircase is often enhanced by the light radiating from a skylight, a lamp, or even a chandelier on a long chain. The steps of the staircase, if not of white stone or marble, and especially in the Nice district, are made of ceramic tiles, whether in country or town houses. The riser is of cement, often coated in dark brown plaster. Although the hardest oak wood was used for the noses of the steps, it has still usually worn away, becoming hollowed out in front of the tiles.

WALLS

There has been a dramatic shift away from the use of the plain distemper or whitewash that was common twenty years ago. Considered capable of curing all the evils of damaged and dilapidated walls, this used to be applied wherever wallpaper was not considered suitable. Now there has been a move into textured walls, rag-rolling, sponging, polished, aged, or limewashed coatings, in all of which ocher is the dominant color. Once the ocher shades used were darker, the best known being burnt sienna. That was until the discovery of the riches of the area around Roussillon, a hilltop village in northern Luberon, near Gordes—it quickly became known as "France's answer to the Painted Desert."

Near here, at Rustrel or Gargas, is situated the only place in France where ocher is still extracted, and it is here that Jean Faucon, the studio potter from Apt, gets his mixed earth. The proportion of iron oxide in the clay gives it the twelve distinctive shades of solid color, which do not easily bleach in the sun. That is why the painters working on exterior walls have to warn their clients not to expect the color to fade.

Ocher is a yellow sand, usually deriving its color from the presence of hydrated iron oxides; it has to be heated to turn red again. After it has been baked dry, the ocher is ground to a golden powder and packed into paper sacks for shipment.

This industry flourished in the 1920s, but suffered from the arrival on the market of synthetic ochers. However, a love of the authentic won the day,

PAGES 80 & 81:
Whether they have simple stone or brick steps, tiled risers, or a double spiral, Provençal staircases are always spectacular.

FACING PAGE:
The former ocher quarries of Roussillon (closed in 1930) were unable to keep up with demand, and products based on natural pigments continue to be popular.

LEFT:
Interior walls are often painted with distemper tinted with ocher pigments from the quarries at Rustrel and Gargas in the Luberon, where shades of ocher range from pale yellow to deep red.

FACING PAGE:
The distemper can also be tinted with azure, as in the blue bedroom of the Château de Lourmarin.

PAGES 86 & 87:
A few examples of shades of ocher, and the art of capturing light.

and there is currently more demand than can be met for ocher pigments. There are twelve different shades of ocher, from pale yellow to black oxide, so whether used pure or mixed, the palette is almost infinite. A wall under a staircase, or a whole living room apart from the ceiling could be painted in red ocher, a color scheme that can be seen in Old Nice in houses in the Genoese style.

Bedrooms are often painted in pale ocher, the color of the rising sun, which is both relaxing and refreshing. This is contrasted with olive green or burnt sienna, colors repeated in the floor tiles.

As for kitchens, natural sienna or dark yellow ocher colors give them character, as long as the floors have pale terra-cotta or white tiles. Anyone lucky enough to have an old floor with large tiles should choose a pale ocher shade for the walls and ceiling.

Kitchen and bathroom walls become a blaze of color thanks to the multicolored earthenware tiles made by the craftsmen of Salernes. The walls and floors are paneled with tiles, framing small, brightly colored squares of plain tiling, or tiles of various different colors decorated with fruits, flowers, or landscapes, to match the frieze that surrounds them.

FLOORING

Marble used for floors does not come exclusively from Italy. Although the floors of the Château de Barbentane, in all their extraordinary variety, were laid in 1774 by Neapolitan craftsmen, there were other practitioners, such as Bernard Virgile Mazzetty, who came from the Tessine in Switzerland and settled in Avignon in 1740. He founded a family business that lasted for three generations, spanning a century, and Mazzetty floors can be found throughout the region, especially in Nîmes, Carpentras, Aix-en-Provence, and Avignon.

The earliest tiles were of unglazed terra-cotta and measured thirteen square inches (33 sq. cm). They were used for the flooring of the local Roman houses and have never been bettered. Many homeowners haunt architectural recyclers to get pink terra-cotta floor tiles, worn down by just the right amount, to be laid in wide expanses. Earthenware tiles are cosy and welcoming with their soft patina and varied shades. Salernes is the center of the tile-making industry, a village in which a group of craftsmen have created the Terre de Salernes label of authenticity. In addition to the classic, indispensable hexagonal tiles—small

FACING PAGE:
Marble and terra-cotta tiles often adorn floors, as here in the Château de Gignac.

88

LEFT:
Tomettes (small hexagonal or square floor tiles) were invented in the mid-nineteenth century by the potters of Moustiers, who had discovered Salernes clay.

FACING PAGE:
The soberness of the flooring in this living room at the Château de Barbentane may be surprising in comparison with the lavish decoration, but in fact the painted furniture is typically rustic.

PAGES 92 & 93:
Terra-cotta tiles like this are easy to maintain: waxing with a red wax twice a year is all that is needed. Tiles made from colored cement or varnished terra-cotta should be cleaned with a little soapy water, then rinsed thoroughly.

TERRA-COTTA TILES HAVE AN AUTHENTIC QUALITY THAT ENABLES THEM TO BE MATCHED WITH AN ENDLESS VARIETY OF STYLES AND COLORS.

for bedrooms, larger for the ground floor—and unglazed terra-cotta squares, there are the jewel-bright, glazed squares in a rainbow of colors, which have a thousand uses, from flooring to wallcovering, in kitchens and bathrooms. A checkerboard of matte-glazed black-and-white tiles, with or without splashes of color, is particularly effective against plain white walls.

In fact, tiling was introduced quite recently into Provence. The Château de Lourmarin, in southern Luberon, built in the early seventeenth century, had only four rooms of brick floor tiles. The *tomette*, the brightly colored square tile typical of Provence, was "invented" by local craftsmen in the late nineteenth century, at a time when floors and staircases were mostly covered in wooden planking. This explains why, previously, the ground floors of the grand houses were covered with marble and the upper floors with parquet.

The tiled flooring industry is now flourishing, and has made extraordinary strides since the 1960s, when Jean Boutal invented a machine for manufacturing *tomettes*. In 1965 his son opened the first large factory at Port Grimaud. Attractive tiles are also manufactured in Aubagne, Apt, and Biot.

There is nothing lovelier than handmade terra-cotta tiling such as the "pavés de Salernes" produced by Pierre Basset. These are compositions of shapes in various shades of faded pink, assembled in a mosaic, in a rose formation, and in tapestry patterns. There are also handmade square tiles measuring from six to twelve inches (14–30 cm), which can be laid with or without grouting to create a range of patterns in "rustic sienna."

Terra-cotta is the most sensual of all the construction materials used in the house; for flooring to be perfect, it should be a pleasure to run over it barefoot!

THE GARDEN

LIVING OUTDOORS

As much time as possible is spent outdoors, for meals,
siestas, and special occasions. The only sounds
are the buzzing of the bees in the lavender bushes
and the gentle trickling of a fountain.

PAGE 96:
This terrace, shaded by
large trees and cooled by the
presence of water, belongs
to the Villa Gallici, a luxury
hotel in Aix-en-Provence.

FACING PAGE:
The play of sun and shade
on this long, sheltered
terrace in the Alpilles
makes it a wonderful
summer living room.

The garden is an important part of the Provençal home and daily life. Houses
are south facing, so even in January, if the day is sunny, one can sit outside on
a bench next to a wall that is slightly warm. It is also possible, on days without wind, to breakfast in the sun at the stone table that is always there and
impervious to bad weather. When summer comes, there is plenty of shade,
often from plane trees. Armchairs and garden furniture are brought out, the
geraniums and nasturtiums provide cascades of bright color, and the orange
and lemon trees planted in big pots decorate the terrace. It is the season for
outdoor eating at colorful tables, enjoying pitchers of ice-cold rosé wine, and
using brightly colored flatware matched with cotton napkins. Barefoot on the
terra-cotta tiles, one surveys the garden and says to oneself that the geraniums need deadheading and the begonia, which has spread too quickly, needs
cutting back, "maybe today, or else tomorrow."

TERRACES

Whether a château, *bastide*, *mas*, or townhouse, every house has this transi-
tional space between the rather private interior and the garden. The terrace is
laid out in front of the building, and is used as an extension of the living quarters as soon as the weather permits. It is a sort of summer living room, shady,
paved, flowery, decorated, and carefully laid out; a kind of ante-chamber to
the house. It completes the image provided by the façades, and is a foretaste
of the style of the interior, its harmony and authenticity.

A *mas* usually has a driveway leading to it from one side, a dirt road lined
with trees, while *bastides* have handsome avenues leading up to them at right
angles to the main entrance. The grounds of the Château de Florans, at which

LEFT:
An abundance of old roses enlivens the severe stone paving of the terrace.

FACING PAGE:
The inviting comfort of a hammock contrasted with the starkness of a stone bench: the paradox of the Provençal climate is seen here in the relaxing garden of the Villa Saint-Louis, a *chambre d'hôte* in Lourmarin.

PAGES 102–3:
The arbor provides enough shade for guests at this house; the parasol serves simply to protect them from twigs and ants falling from the overhanging greenery.

the La Roque-d'Anthéron Piano Festival is held, is an extreme example, with its double row of plane trees with a grassy expanse in between. A row of sequoias has been planted at right angles to the drive, to offset the oval ornamental pond and the flight of steps leading to the terrace.

In humbler homes, which are often built on slightly raised ground to allow rainwater to drain away, a low wall separates the terrace from the garden, which is on a slightly lower level. The garden is a place for walking through and around, for growing flowers and vegetables. It has ornamental ponds, statues, and paths edged with lavender. There may be flowerbeds and boxwood topiary work inherited from the Renaissance, of which there are extraordinary examples at the Château d'Ansouis near Cucuron, in the southern Luberon. If the garden is on a hillside, an embankment built of stone (*restanque*) may border the terrace. It will be topped with planters containing flowers or shrubs, separating it from the olive trees with their changing colors, or the summer opulence of the fruit trees.

Like the house, the terrace is more sophisticated than it first appears. Banks of flowers blooming against the frontage; the large table under a plane tree; the chairs and stone benches placed to take advantage of the winter sun and the summer shade; the terra-cotta vases containing brilliantly colored geraniums; the citrus trees with their dark green, shiny leaves; the trellis covered with flowering vines: all these elements seem to have been thrown together by accident—or to have been there for ever. The paving is an important feature, once again created by the skill of the local craftsmen.

Architects are required to ensure that the paving used for the terrace adjoining the house harmonizes with the building itself. In the handsome eighteenth-century *bastides*, especially those used as wineries where the ground floor is used exclusively for storing wine, as at the Château de Mesclances at La Crau in the Var, the terrace is a large area in proportion to the dimensions of the façade, covering the entire width of the building. The same design is used for the Mediterranean villas; these are built on piles, so the ground floor is unoccupied. The terraces here are paved with large terra-cotta or stoneware tiles, or in textured, mossy, flattened cobblestones. The faded colors are well-matched to the smooth plaster and ornamentation of the façade. The terrace is often separated from the garden by a stone balustrade, and is shaded by the frontage of the house. It often opens onto a large central stone flight of

FACING PAGE:
The foliage of the olive tree and the gentle slant of the lavender testify to this fragrant meadow's exposure to the Mistral.

PAGES 106–7:
This fine, classical-style *bastide*, situated in the center of the village of Lourmarin, has a terrace with balusters on the first floor, over what were once professional warehouses and workshops.

LEFT:
Outdoor furniture is mostly simple in style and made from wrought iron: folding tables and chairs that are easy to move around and put away.

FACING PAGE:
Nurseryman Jean-Marie Rey has chosen to cover his pergola, which overlooks his garden in La Londe-les-Maures, with very fine *canisse* (Provence cane screening), which lets air and light through.

steps leading to clumps of trees and a water feature. This leads to a majestic avenue of plane trees, which links the main road, the vineyard, the cellars, and the residence.

In the *mas* and village houses, whose secret gardens are invisible from the street, the terrace has an important role to play. The paving is often very intricate, and can be a genuine work of art.

There is often an avenue of flat stones, laid in geometric patterns, or fieldstone, as at the Serre de La Madone, Menton. All around the house, and along the width of the façade, there is a paved area designed mainly to allow water to run off quickly, since in Provence it rains in short, heavy bursts.

Two attractive paving techniques are used for paths or avenues in level gardens. *Calpinage* is the name given to brickwork, laid on edge and often in a herringbone pattern like a parquet floor. Over the years it acquires a rich flora of grasses and moss, which grow in the gaps between the bricks. The pale green blends with the pink of the terra-cotta in a combination of muted tones. Narrow channels, the same depth as the bricks used, efficiently drain the rainwater away. *Calades*, an Italian feature, consist of expanses of river pebbles in contrasting colors, ranging from black to white, assembled on the spot in curving and round patterns, and fixed in place by packed earth covered in a thin screed of mortar. They are also used in the garden itself to mark the paths that wind between low boxwood hedges, as at the Château d'Ansouis. These *calades* also decorate the forecourts of many major buildings in Provence, such as that of the Musée de l'Annonciade in Saint-Tropez and those in the old quarter of Nice.

Beyond the avenue and the sidewalk, the terrace is simply covered in grass, or in fine, white, round river gravel. The latter is often preferred for paths and for the areas set aside for tables, benches, and recliners. For the garden of La Louve at Bonnieux, blue pebbles were chosen; their muted colors harmonize with the various stonework features—stone slabs, edging, benches, and troughs, interspersed with boxwood hedging and hollyhocks. The surrounds of the ornamental ponds and water features are usually paved with large stone slabs. Over time these have turned the same color as the statuary and the fountains, features that are so welcome in a land where the drought lasts for months at a time.

FACING PAGE:
A *calade* (stepped path) made from pebbles from the Crau (once submerged by the Rhône) leads up to this *bastide* in the Alpilles.

PAGES 112–13:
The carefully cleared trunk of this old mulberry tree, which stands in front of the *mas* belonging to landscape architect Alex Dingwall-Main in Lacoste, is a wonderful, natural work of art, sculpted by time.

IT WOULD BE DIFFICULT TO LIVE HERE WITHOUT THE SOUND OF WATER AND THE FRESHNESS IT BRINGS TO THE GARDEN.

WATER FEATURES

Water is an indispensable feature in our gardens, the symbol of refreshment and a sign of life in the sweltering heat of summer. It is hard to live here without being able to listen to the splash of water; it also offers refreshment for domestic animals, birds, and hedgehogs. The nurseryman Jean-Marie Rey, a specialist in Mediterranean plants, has installed large glazed water jars in his private garden, almost adjacent to the gravel terrace. They are planted with water lilies and are a novel way of introducing a water feature.

The value of a house, especially a *mas*, whose family and land demands heavy water consumption, has always been measured in terms of the abundance of well water, the presence of a spring, or the closeness of a river. Remember the story *Jean de Florette* by Marcel Pagnol, in which a blocked spring leads a father of a family to ruin and death.

Water was yet another external trapping of wealth for the châteaux and *bastides* inspired by Versailles, and the fountain-maker had an important job, at least until the waters of the Canal de Provence began to irrigate all the local farms and made it unnecessary to capture and store water. But in Provence, water is never wasted or lost. The water of the fountains and basins travels around in a closed circuit. The water comes from water butts and tanks situated high up on the retaining walls, on the old water-tower principle. This provides the water pressure for the kitchen faucet before running down into the washtub and troughs, and it is then used to water the kitchen garden and the rest of the plants.

A reasonably large pond or pool surrounded by trees will provide shade and coolness through evaporation. It is easy to find a place for a fountain, even in the smallest garden. A waterspout in the shape of a mask and a basin can be acquired from sellers of recycled materials, and lends style to the plainest exterior. A fashion for statuary arrived alongside that for pools. In the seventeenth century, the Genoese became wealthy by growing olive trees and grapevines. They used their money to build *bastides* with elaborate gardens, copied from Italian Renaissance originals. The local inhabitants adapted these to their taste, making them one of the typical features of the region.

FACING PAGE:
The Relais de la Magdeleine—formerly the château of the Marquis d'Albertas, and today a luxury hotel in Gémenos— has a classical-style pond with stone edging and pillar.

PAGES 116-17:
Visitors to the Jardins d'Albertas at Bouc-bel-Air, near Aix-en-Provence, are delighted to discover this long pool lined with plane trees leading to a cool grotto.

ON TERRACES AND IN GARDENS, LIFE FLOWS BY
PEACEFULLY IN THE SHADE OF PERGOLAS
AND ARBORS, WHICH TEMPT YOU TO IDLENESS.

GARDEN FURNITURE

Although the sun is welcome from October to May, at other times of the year it is vital to live in the shade. Deciduous trees are particularly suitable for planting—ideal for the purpose are plane trees, Spanish chestnuts, false acacias or black locus trees, or a row of mulberry trees or oaks, such as at La Mignarde, at Aix-en-Provence.

The natural shade is supplemented by the trellises and pergolas attached to the façade, the most famous being the muscat-grape trellis that gave its name to the house in Saint-Tropez owned by the writer Colette. Pergolas and arbors also provide shade on the terrace or in the garden. They are often roofed with canes that filter light and air and throw a pattern of sun splashes onto the paving stones. They are at their best when covered with wisteria, which flowers in early spring even before the foliage appears, as long as it is on a southfacing wall. Bougainvillea and jasmine flourish in southern Provence and throughout the Nice district, climbing riotously around wooden or bamboo poles, as in the garden of Val Rahmeh, in Menton. Even the humblest villa boasts decorative wrought-ironwork, trellises, and arbors.

Many antique dealers specialize in old wrought-iron furniture. It can also be found at antique fairs and street markets, especially on the Isle-sur-la-Sorgue, or it can be bought from local forges. Modern, simplified ironwork designs harmonize perfectly with the style of old farmhouses and country houses.

EARTHENWARE POTS AND VASES

Bright colors prevail in Provence. They can be found in the stucco, fabrics, walls and, of course, the garden. Terra-cotta pots contribute a reddish-pink, a faded rose, and the bright green and ocher of the glazes, as well as coming in an infinite variety of shapes: flowerpots, potbellied urns, and vases on steady, round bases; stone and earthenware jars of every provenance, once used for storing preserves and perishable foods and now used for growing plants. This profusion of containers is designed solely to satisfy the Provençal love of flowers.

FACING PAGE:
A terrace paved with butt-jointed stone slabs, shaded by an arbor: perfect for summer meals.

PAGES 120–21:
From the end of winter, the wisteria lays its bluish screen over the pergola, while still letting the sun's rays pass through onto the terrace, which overlooks a terraced garden created by Jean Mus above the valley of Grasse.

POTS, VASES, AND JARS FROM BIOT AND ANDUZE ADD THEIR NOTE OF COLOR TO GARDENS AND TERRACES.

The oldest known jars come from Biot. Some are glazed inside and were used to hold oil, wine, or brine; others are of plain, unglazed terra-cotta. Jars are still made in Biot, at the Poterie Provençale for instance. They may be wide, oval, or potbellied, and they stand in terrace corners, or beside garden paths overflowing with pelargoniums and petunias. They may be antique, or merely old, and they have a patina that makes them look as if they have stood in the garden since time immemorial.

For more than a hundred years, the Ravel potteries near Aubagne have been extracting a yellowish clay from their quarries to give their large pots decorated with garlands and their fluted jars a pale, almost faded look and a softness to the touch that makes them instantly recognizable. Large, rustic pots, in the classic, almost cylindrical shape, with a wide base, are often planted with shaped boxwood or pittosporum.

The big pots known as *vases d'Anduze* are used to hold all types of plants, but especially orange trees. These are the type of pots that were used at Versailles, though there they were much more elaborate. They are made almost exclusively by two potteries, Les Enfants de Boisset in Anduze, and the Poterie de La Madeleine at Tornac. The shape is inspired by the Medici vases, and the decoration—flower or fruit garlands—runs around the famous coat of arms that is the mark of their authenticity. When they are genuine antiques, the peeling glaze reveals a pale layer of slip covering the terra-cotta, on top of which the green, yellow, or brown jasper is laid before the final transparent glaze known as alquifoux is applied by the potters of Dieulefit. These pots are one of the most typical ornaments of the gardens of Provence.

While Biot jars and Ravel pots, which are almost velvety to the touch, line the retaining walls or stand beside the low hedges of the garden paths, the *vases d'Anduze* are just as attractive in the sunshine, standing alone in a corner of the terrace, under leaf fronds, where the light plays on the bright glaze as it filters through the foliage, as at the Clos du Peyronnet, one of the loveliest gardens in Menton. They make a treasured gift for weddings or any other celebration, because the material and colors represent the quintessence of Provençal country crafts.

PAGES 126–27:
The fig harvest—the Provençal variety Violette de Solliès has its own *appellation d'origine contrôlée*—in a lush garden where two old olive jars serve as the base of a table.

LEFT:
At Ramatuelle, a door opens onto a little flower garden with potted plants.

FACING PAGE:
The terrace of the Château Val Joanis—a winery near Aix-en-Provence that is open to the public—is paved with round river pebbles from the Durance.

PAGES 130–31:
The owners of this house in Gordes have chosen traditional materials for their terrace: gravel on the ground and thick *canisse* (Provence cane screening) on the pergola.

DECORATIVE FEATURES

PROVENÇAL STYLE

It used to be a local tradition to order sets of furniture
for bedrooms or dining rooms, as in the eighteenth century.
Regrettably, this matching furniture has long been dispersed.

POLISHED AND PAINTED WOOD FURNITURE

The French naval base at Toulon was the source of a distinctive Provençal style that emerged in the eighteenth century. For ships' carpenters and cabinetmakers skilled at making balustrades and bulwarks for the poop deck, making chests of drawers and closets to order was child's play, and an excellent way of supplementing their meager wages. The wealthy merchants of Marseilles had been in the habit of ordering their furniture from Paris, and the local aristocracy, who lived mainly in the capital, Aix-en-Provence, did not want to be outdone. They wanted their furniture to be as elegant as that at the French court. Local firms therefore began commissioning ship's carpenters to copy expensive furniture. In fact this showed that Parisian cabinetmakers had much to learn from Provence.

The woods used by these skilled woodworkers, carpenters, and cabinet-makers—as well as on a semi-industrial scale by the furniture factories of Marseilles—are always the same. They include the finest walnut, which is redder in hue in Haute-Provence, with darker markings. All the furniture was made of solid wood; veneering was almost unknown. Fruitwood furniture, made of cherry and pear, is also common. Unlike other regions, in which quality furniture uses oak supports, in Provence all the furniture used soft wood supports of pine or limewood, the latter being used to make the elaborate frames gilded with gold leaf for large mirrors. Sideboards and commodes were rarely marble-topped, except when specially commissioned.

Sculptors designed, classified, and described patterns and detailing in furniture, woodwork, mirrors, wrought and cast iron, stucco, pictures, and metalwork. Bernard Turau, known as Toro, from Toulon, was a pupil of the famous sculptor Pierre Puget (1620–94). Toro decorated many mansions in Aix and

LEFT:
A large bust of an Arlesian girl—the Provençal firm Souleïado's tribute to the painter Léo Lelée.

FACING PAGE:
In the bay of a double window, this late eighteenth- or early nineteenth-century, rush-seated *chapeau de gendarme* settee is the polished walnut version of the eighteenth-century painted *radassié*.

THE WOODS USED BY CABINETMAKERS ARE THE SAME EVERYWHERE, OFTEN BEAUTIFUL WALNUT WITH COLORED VEINS.

Marseilles; he left behind numerous plates, drawings, and notebooks that were copied by all the craftsmen in the region. This is the origin of the so-called Arlesian style, often considered to be the only truly Provençal style of furniture.

A distinctive feature of the Arlesian style is that the crosspieces of closets, sideboards, and chests of drawers are all carved with a cockleshell in the center; this is flanked on both sides with swags and garlands. This style became known in Paris as rocaille. If the crosspieces are not decorated in this style, they may be *décor à la soupière* (decorated like a soup tureen), with the uprights covered in laurel leaves, roses, olive branches, or acanthus leaves. Little bureaus with a drop leaf and two drawers, and sideboards whose upper sections have sliding doors are also typical. The upper section of the sideboard is set back, allowing flatware and china to be arranged on top of the lower half. The sliding doors flank a central "tabernacle."

Storage furniture is sometimes built in, such as closets under a staircase, but may still have beautifully carved doors. The living room may contain a two-piece bookcase, or a corner cabinet may be fitted into the masonry. The dresser, as such, does not exist: crockery is stored in tall, closed, two-piece cabinets, or in chests topped with a matching set of shelves that are simply placed on top. To enable the top of the chest to be used for storage or as a dresser, it can be attached to the wall or placed on the ground. There are several types of shelving, including the *estagnié*, which was used for displaying pewterware; the *escudilié* for china; and the *veiriau*: the bottom part of this was for carafes and flasks, and was protected by a gallery of turned wood, and the upper shelves were for glassware.

Armoires are heavily carved and incised, with double doors. They sometimes have bulbous frontages and curving sides. Until the eighteenth century, they were finished at the top with an overhanging cornice of the shape known in French as *chapeau de gendarme*. Later the cornice is flatter, with richly carved front rails, deer-hoof feet, or volutes resting on a wedge-shaped foot to ensure stability. An expensive wardrobe would have four sculpted feet—plain back feet are considered to indicate poor quality—and would be lined with a flowered cotton print, attached by upholstery stitches concealed with braiding stuck to the surface. Such an armoire was a traditional marriage gift. The Arlesian marriage armoire is the most highly sought after, both for the beauty of the decoration and for its emotional charge.

FACING PAGE:
This armoire in pale walnut is typical of late eighteenth-century Provençal style.

FACING PAGE:
The pale oak parquet
flooring, rugs, and so-called
"chinoiserie" wallpaper in
the living room are evidence
of the exceptional quality of
the interior furnishings of
this noble town residence,
now a hotel—La Mirande—in
the heart of Avignon.

RIGHT:
A Louis XIV "crossbow"
commode made from
fruitwood with a peach-
blossom marble top. The
scrolls above the feet were
invented by cabinetmakers
from Arles.

PAGES 142 & 143:
Buffets à glissants:
sideboards on top of which
a compartment with sliding
doors was placed. This
opening system freed up
most of the top surface of the
lower part of the sideboard,
which could then serve as
a dresser. The color and
quality of the walnut were
obtained by means of a
special drying process. In
Provence, the trees were
felled amid great ceremony,
but timber was also floated
in to Marseilles.

THE TRADITION OF PAINTED FURNITURE PREVAILS IN PROVENCE, WHERE CONTEMPORARY ARTISTS USE THEIR SKILLS TO CREATE HIGHLY DESIRABLE PIECES.

FACING PAGE:
A manor-house kitchen with painted pale wood furniture and a stove fitted into the fireplace alcove.

PAGE 146:
A Louis XIV marriage armoire at the Musée de Grasse, decorated with roses, musical instruments, parchments, and a flower-trimmed hat: the cabinetmaker who sculpted it was hugely creative as well as talented!

PAGE 147:
The *manjadou* quickly surpassed its function as a pantry to become a piece of furniture in which to display fine flatware, in the semi-open top section. These days it makes an ideal jam cupboard.

The most sought-after commodes are either in the "crossbow" pattern, with a slightly bowed front and central mullion, echoed in modern furniture, or those with a single or double bow-front, known as a "tomb commode." The two-drawer chests on feet, known as *sauteuses*, are a specialty of Provence. They are lighter in shape and decoration than the commodes, are made of fruitwood, and are elegant enough to add chic to a large reception room. In large items of furniture, the Transition Style is expressed mainly in the commodes with bowed feet and flat-fronted drawers, a forerunner of the classic simplicity of Louis XVI style.

Bureaus in a style known as *dos d'âne* (donkey back), halfway between a secretaire writing desk and a commode, have two deep drawers decorated with moldings and carvings, and were made in the plain of Arles. The interiors feature a set of miniature drawers, and often included a secret compartment.

Chests and sideboards also had double doors, and are sometimes fitted with drawers. They are often bow-fronted or with crossbow fronts. In the best quality furniture, the tops are of a single piece of wood; where the grain was palest the wood was reputed to be least sturdy, so it was placed behind the top. The structure and decoration remain unchanged in a matching upper section, which is always laid flat on the surface of the lower section. The upper piece may consist of a set of two or three drawers narrower than the one on which it rests, or a set of shelves, or even a second, taller chest, topped with a *chapeau-de-gendarme* cornice. This piece of furniture has been favored in modest country homes since Louis XIII (seventeenth century), when it featured a lozenge decoration. The following century was the heyday of Provençal style, when the sideboard with sliding doors in the so-called Arlesian style was the most representative of the fine furniture of the region.

The bread box, which was originally designed to sit on the floor, is actually more usually hung on the wall. This makes it easier to admire its elaborate carving, turned spindles, decorative metalwork, and the wooden pinnacles at the top, beneath which a wheat sheaf spilled from a basket. The *panetière* was made from a silky walnut with a close grain, carefully aged then polished regularly to preserve the patina.

The *manjadou* is a delightful pantry; it looks like a small cabinet, with a lower and an upper door pierced with turned spindles to aerate the inside. Thanks to its lovely proportions, it has now graduated from the kitchen.

Small items of furniture that were used in every room in the house were also made locally, many in Aix-en-Provence, where the houses were large and the citizens wealthy, and thus able to afford these little gems.

The dainty drop-leaf *dos d'âne* secretaires and sloping, single-drawer desks have a classic simplicity with their four tall legs ending in deer-hoof feet, and their sawn crosspieces. The flap, with curved edges in Louis XV style, later became rectangular, and sometimes had boxwood stringing. When the drop leaf is opened, resting on its slides, the gilt leather-covered interior is revealed, consisting of little drawers and pigeonholes.

Gaming tables and writing tables, the best of which are made of fruitwood, are in the same spirit as the secretaires: delicate, with curved lines. The gaming tables have a little circular extension at each corner, on which to place gaming chips, and are finished with wooden beading. Writing tables are leather covered, and may have a rail around three sides.

Marble-topped, cabriolet-legged bedside tables, miniature side tables with a simple crosspiece, polished wooden chests of drawers decorated with gilding and wrought ironwork, are all indispensable items of furniture for a classic Provençal interior. They match the rest of the decor, introducing a lighter note in contrast to the heavy items of furniture in solid walnut.

Gilding has always been in favor in Provence, and is used on picture frames, console tables, moldings, barometers, and mirrors, usually on frames carved from limewood by master craftsmen. One mirror in the Hôtel de l'Europe in Avignon dates from the French Régence (1715–23), and is a classic example of all the Provençal types of decoration including "Bérain rings" and fluted pilasters.

The Provençal mirrors known as "Beaucaire mirrors" were not made in Beaucaire but were sold at the big fair held annually in the town. A list of the gilders and sculptors shows most of them to be operating in Avignon and the Comtat Venaissin, Toulon, Marseilles, Apt, Carpentras, or Nîmes. All these mirrors are decorated in rocaille style. They have become very rare and are very valuable, especially when the mirror surface contains mercury and the frame has never needed regilding.

The tradition of painted furniture is by no means new, and was not restricted to the countryside. Even in town, chairs and small closets were decorated to match the matte-painted wood paneling. Walnut was plentiful, but this noble

FACING PAGE:
A commode decorated with naive stenciled frescoes. The wooden drawer knobs and the lack of brass keyholes reveal the rustic nature of this nevertheless charming piece of furniture.

LEFT:
Corner cupboards provide additional storage and often consist of a simple façade masking shelves fixed directly to the walls.

FACING PAGE:
In the eighteenth century, the beautiful silk brocade cushions on this matching *radassié* and armchair against the back wall would have invited the ladies to rest at the end of a meal, while the men went outside to smoke.

PAGES 152 & 153:
The opulence of the Provençal style reaches its peak at the Château de Barbentane: gilded mirrors with foliage scrolls and flower motifs framing the famous Arlesian cockleshell, and an inlaid "tomb commode" with a marble top and bronze rocaille and Roi-Soleil ornamentation.

wood was never painted. Furniture made of solid wood that is polished and waxed, and in reality given a light coat of French polish to protect it and give it a patina, is usually of cherrywood.

It is possible, in view of the difficulty of finding authentic pieces of furniture, to commission them from a traditional cabinetmaker, who will also be able to restore a genuine piece to its original condition. Such craftsmen create authentic pieces, made of the same wood and using the same tools and techniques as in the past. Doursin at Pernes and Roehrig in Antibes are perpetuating the presence of true Provençal furniture in our homes.

CHAIRS

The typical "Provençal chair" can be found everywhere. It is made of walnut or mulberry, a plentiful wood that does not rot. The back is curved and has three bowed stretchers. Sometimes, but only on painted chairs, the stretcher may be shaped like an ear of wheat, and is called *à la gerbe*. The seat is usually made of two types of rush, the weft being of *sagne*, a pale green reed found in the Camargue, and the top of a gold-colored reed, sometimes decorated with bands of green *sagne*.

In the city, upright chairs and large armchairs are made of polished walnut, carved and upholstered in silk, cotton piqué, velvet, or damask. The Provençal chair reached the height of elegance in the eighteenth century. One can find handsome painted, straight-backed armchairs of the Régence period, and armchairs of polished walnut.

Rush-bottomed chairs are always popular in the country. The seat is often rushed with *aufo*, also known as *feuilles de Sparte*, a grass found on the banks of the River Rhône. Then there is the two-, three-, or four-seater settee, which has a rush bottom, stretchers carved with flowers, and a curved back. This is the *radassié* or *radassière*, meaning a chair on which one lazes around. The name for this light and elegant seating comes from the word *radassa*, which means lazybones. In Provence it is often used incorrectly to describe less comfortable benches that were mainly used at the table.

FACING PAGE:
The famous shell "invented" by the Arlesians appeared everywhere, as here on the back of a rustic armchair. Its success was such that it was adopted by Versailles and became the symbol of the Régence style.

PAGES 156 & 157:
A few examples of old Provençal seating: the width of the seat—as required by the triple petticoats of the ladies—is typical and made the seats of the *radassiés* comfortable to sit in. The backs of these chairs, by contrast, were so upright that no one nowadays would choose to sit on them, but they were redeemed by their aesthetic qualities.

COTTONS, QUILTS, AND FURNISHING FABRICS

The story of Provençal fabrics begins in the port of Marseilles, where ships arrived from the Levant in the days of the Ottoman Empire, discharging huge bales of cloth. The imported fabrics included Egyptian cotton, Syrian cloth, and delicate muslins from India, printed in paisley designs or floral patterns.

No sooner had the fabrics crossed the threshold of the Provençal home than they were turned into patterned mattresses and quilts, upholstery, frills, and furbelows. French windows were curtained in a single sheet of fluttering muslin, brilliant cloths adorned the tables, and brightly colored, well-padded cushions were added to armchairs. Beds were covered in plain silk bedspreads, or elaborately quilted comforters, decorated with rose or lilac patterns. Finally, there was the cradle, which was swathed in a pure white muslin of the finest weave—soft and delicate as a spider's web so as not to scratch the delicate skin of a baby—the quintessence of the embroiderer's skill.

OLD AND NEW FABRICS

The history of fabric in Provence is a cosmopolitan one. It was a Jew, one of those banished from Andalusia in 1497 as part of the Expulsion from Spain, who began manufacturing silken cloth in Marseilles. The Spaniards came to the city to teach the art of velvet weaving, and the Venetians that of making scarlet blankets. The Armenians shared their techniques for improving the quality of prints. Marseilles exported American cochineal to Constantinople, and Languedoc woolen cloth, as well as gold and silver cloth, to the Portuguese, Italians, and Persians. It was an extremely lively commercial center. So it is hardly surprising that the fabrics used to decorate Provençal homes arrived in the late seventeenth century from the Near East. They often bore the name of the cities of their manufacture, and these have been retained, though in rather distorted form, as tarlatan, organdie, calico, nansouk, malle molle, peking, bayadère, taffeta, chintz, mohair, and so on.

Most of these were cotton fabrics, processed in various ways depending on the provenance. The printed muslins worn by Indian women can be found all over the subcontinent; very fine white percale was imported from Pondicherry,

FACING PAGE:
The upper surface of a quilt is often made of printed fabric, while the reverse side is plain, as in this child's bed dressed with a quilt featuring a splendid rambling plant motif, designed by Florence Maeght.

LEFT:
Color samples for a quilt by the firm Souleïado.

FACING PAGE:
Quilts by Souleïado, which has recently relaunched its range of household linens using eighteenth-century printing plates—an exclusive collection.

PAGE 162:
This armchair (top, left) is upholstered with the Cupidon design by Les Olivades. The collection of quilts and *boutis* from Souleïado in Tarascon (top, right and bottom, left and right) constitutes an important heritage, as can be seen in these nineteenth-century examples.

PAGE 163:
In the company's workshops, colors are evolved based on carefully preserved engraved patterns.

THE INVENTION OF THE PROVENÇAL STYLE: BUSY PATTERNS OF STYLIZED FLOWERS, PAIRED WITH WHAT HAS BECOME KNOWN AS *LES BONNES HERBES*—LITTLE FLOWERS, OLIVE BRANCHES, AND BEES.

a French colony in India, as were the prints and painted, embroidered, warp-dyed, and striped fabrics. Two types of pattern were typical, regardless of the fabric. The first were the Persian patterns, known in the English-speaking world as paisley, designs of Arab origin represented on Persian carpets; the second were the Indian patterns, mainly taken from the illustrations in the herbals brought to the Moghul court by the Jesuits.

These cottons, known in French as *indiennes*, were made into curtains, pillows, valances, bed-hangings, and drapes, and used to upholster armchairs and line clothes closets. But since this merchandise was imported it was very costly, and protectionist measures soon banned its importation anyway. The way was clear to developing locally made fabrics of the same type.

Marseilles became famous for its painted cloth. Tapestries of cotonine (a mixture of linen and cotton) painted with tempera decorated the walls of the *bastides* and châteaux of the région. Designs included golden medallions on a cream background, greenery, and yellow and blue monochrome landscapes. Marseilles cloth, cotton printed with Indian patterns, made great use of red, a dye brought from Andrianople to Marseilles by the Armenians. The background color was usually cream or cobalt blue. Cloth-dyers opened workshops in Marseilles, Aix-en-Provence, Avignon, Nîmes, Orange, Tarascon, Toulon, and in the Drôme, and rented the large fields they needed for drying the cloth that had been dyed with madder, a dark red pigment.

The patterns were adapted to a new, Provençal style. In addition to the flowers, designers added fragrant herbs, and branches of olives and grapes, small bouquets, tiny fruits, and bees. Indian pink was replaced by less strident colors, such as the pale green of the olive leaf, or stronger colors such as deep bronze. These were printed on Egyptian percale, an excellent material for making washable *indiennes* with a white or colored background, including a deep blue from Antioch and red from Smyrna.

Other influences were introduced in the nineteenth century. First came the Directoire, with its straight lines, stripes broken with flowers, checks, ovals, and various shades of lavender; then the Empire, with its polka dots. The patterns were always tiny. Napoleon loved them and gave many checker-patterned fabrics to the Empress Josephine.

At the Jourdan workshops at Tarascon, now the Souleïado factory, there are piles of pearwood textile printing blocks in which these patterns are carved. Despite the ravages of the Industrial Revolution, when many of the blocks were burned, forty thousand remain, and they are still used to make fabric to order, when a collector wants cloth printed in the traditional way.

Les Olivades opened at Saint-Étienne-du-Grès in 1818, at the height of the Romantic period. Its fabric colors included faded ocher, an almost silvery green (the eternal search for the color of the olive leaf), and dull pinks, which evoke past times when young women would have chosen them in preparing their trousseau.

Visits to specialist antique sellers, exhibitions at the Château-Gombert in Marseilles, and the collections of many other associations, museums, and châteaux, reveal that, faithful to the original designs, Provençal craftsmen never introduced human figures, animals, or landscapes into their patterns. There might be the occasional bird, and a few mythological scenes in Toile-de-Jouy style, as in certain designs recently revived by Les Olivades. Lavender was not one of the herbs depicted in patterns because its cultivation is of recent date. The representations were always stylized, a trend that became stronger with the advent of modernism.

Provençal fabric designs are enjoying a huge comeback. They are popular throughout the world, but especially in the United States, where the elaborate French quilting technique, which gave rise to American quilts, is particularly admired. The fabrics are made into counterpanes and comforters, table mats, and cushions. Unquilted patterned fabrics use the same color scheme of ocher, red, olive green, and sky blue, and are woven in percale, piqué, linen, and cretonne to decorate the house and to brighten plain fabrics with patterned trim.

The great Provençal weavers of today are Souleïado, Les Olivades, Valdrôme, and Les Indiennes de Nîmes, all of whom produce classic patterned *indiennes* that, in an interior, look like they could have been chosen by a Provençal forebear.

QUILTING AND FURNISHING FABRICS

Quilted fabrics originate from Central Asia, where the winters are bitterly cold and the summers scorchingly hot. Tadjik tribesmen on their donkeys still wear hand-quilted kaftans, whose shabby blue exterior with its pink frogging hides a bright, flower-patterned quilted lining to protect them from the cold.

PAGES 168–69:
This bedroom at the hotel La Mirande in Avignon is furnished with modern fabric in Provençal blood red and gold, like the colors of the Catalan flag.

FACING PAGE:
A marriage *boutis* decorated with palm leaves, flowers, and pearls, created by Rideau de Paris.

QUILTS ARE MADE IN CLOTH PRINTED WITH LARGE PATTERNS, AS WELL AS IN PLAIN SILKS, TAFFETA, MOIRÉS, AND BROCADES.

PAGES 172 & 173:
The *boutis* is Provence's finest creation: made from very fine, close-weave percale, it combines the techniques of padding and quilting. Such pieces require months of work and are created today in the workshops of associations.

FACING PAGE:
Nowadays, the major manufacturers innovate by combining their motifs or by updating their colors, rather than by inventing new designs, as they already have a wealth of patterns in their stores, as is evidenced by Michel Biehn's collection when he was in Isle-sur-la-Sorgue.

In Provence the various ways in which the fabrics were used produced wonderful results. Whether quilted, or used as upholstery fabric or for furnishings (*boutis*), they were all very sought after by collectors.

Quilts are made in cloth printed with large patterns, as well as in plain silks, taffeta, moirés, and brocades. The upper surface would be created in an expensive, patterned fabric, since this would be the side on view, with mattress ticking in striped or plain hemp or silk padding for the underside, and a layer of silk or cotton wadding in between.

When plain fabrics, usually silk, are quilted, the patterns are traditionally elaborate, not leaving a square inch undecorated, and they are often thrown into relief by stump work, the origin of the *boutis*.

Matelassage is a simpler form of quilting, a technique typical of Marseilles, which is used on fragile fabrics that would not withstand heavy quilting. It is also used on fabrics that are so heavily patterned that fancy stitching would not look attractive on them. If it is made entirely of silk, a quilted comforter measuring forty square inches will weigh no more than eight ounces (250 g per sq. m); if it were made of cotton or wool and padded with cotton in the normal way, it would weigh six times more.

Boutis, also known as *broderie emboutie*, is one of the most beautiful of folk arts. The white fabrics are of the finest percale, which should be looked after with great care, since the quality of the fabric is irreplaceable. Small ones were made for cradles to be given as gifts, but they needed to be started even before the mother-to-be was betrothed, because each took more than a thousand hours to make.

Boutis are prepared in the same way as quilting. Once the two thicknesses of fabric and their intermediate wadding have been assembled, the patterns are traced, pricked by hand in double outline, before the thick cotton thread, the *boutis*, is threaded with a bodkin between the pricked-out areas to throw them into relief. The quilting patterns cover the whole fabric in a riot of curlicues, palmetto leaves, artichokes, or geometric shapes. The result is magnificent, all the more astonishing if one examines it against the light.

The work is so meticulous, so delicate, and has become so rare that Provençal *boutis* are now collectors' items, and the term may one day become a registered label or an appellation of origin.

CERAMICS
AND GLASSWARE

Rustic tableware has always been made from terra-cotta.
In 1689, Louis XIV melted down his gold and silver tableware
and began to eat from plates made from faience. And thus began
the golden age of the potters of Marseilles, Varages, and Moustiers.

FACING PAGE:
In her studio at La Colle
sur Loup, Jacqueline
Morabito designs fine
earthenware crockery that
is manufactured at Vallauris
and at Pichon in Uzès. Some
pieces are traditionally
shaped and others highly
innovative, but they all come
exclusively in five or six
shades of white.

Whether standing against the wall in the dining room, or in a large kitchen that can be used for family meals, the dresser might be regarded as an essential item of furniture, even if it is just a simple, modern piece made of pine. Yet in fact the dresser is not part of the Provence inventory of furniture. It is possible to find sideboards on which to display one's best china, or set soup tureens and vegetable dishes. However, it is easier to find an *estagnié*, which was used to display pewter measuring jugs, pitchers, and plates. Every mistress of the house had china she wanted to display, platters and dishes she had inherited or received as gifts, or items she had acquired from antique dealers and china stores. Probably collectable china was hung on the wall in bygone days.

Ceramics—from the Greek word *keramon*, meaning clay—are as old as man himself, and the word is used to describe any object made of terra-cotta, earthenware, pottery, or porcelain. Ceramics are made and sold by a potter.

The earliest pottery kilns have been found in Spain, but it was Faenza in Italy that lent its name to a type of ceramic known as faience. This is made from a pure clay, protected and colored by a glaze. The finest pottery, which reverberates like a tuning fork when flicked with the finger, is a white paste ceramic that is fired twice, then glazed with a transparent lead-based glaze. The red or pinkish color of the clay indicates the presence of iron. The places that have become large centers of production are Apt, Aubagne, Biot, Moustiers, Salernes, Uzès, Vallauris, and Varages.

PAGES 178–79:
In the kitchen at the hotel La Mirande in Avignon, the canning jars are glazed on the inside, as were ancient amphorae used for transporting wine, oil, and fish brine.

FACING PAGE:
Various pieces in glazed terra-cotta, including bowls, oil jars, eighteenth century-style scalloped-edge plates, a water jug, and an olive jar.

RIGHT:
A lovely *pile* (shallow stone sink) in front of the kitchen window at the Mas de Barbut, a *chambre d'hôtes* near Aigues-Mortes.

PAGE 182:
The butler's pantry at the Château de Gignac, near Rustrel: the fine earthenware crockery is stored in the dining room.

PAGE 183:
The contemporary glazed terra-cotta tableware from Biot, Salernes, Villecroze, and Dieulefit should not be confused with fine faience, which makes a clear sound when flicked with a finger.

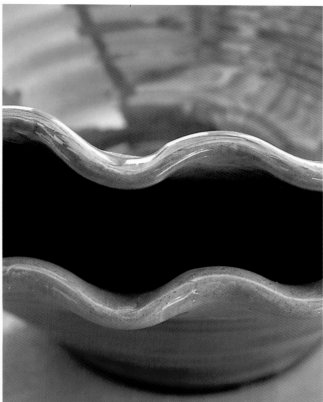

FIRING TURNS CLAY INTO AN ALMOST INDESTRUCTIBLE MATERIAL; IT IS STABLE, CANNOT DISSOLVE, AND CAN LAST FOR CENTURIES UNDAMAGED.

CLAYS AND FIRINGS

Pottery has always been made in the same way. The raw clay is filtered, decanted, and dried. It is then kneaded for a long time in order to remove any air bubbles. Standard shapes are then turned on a potter's wheel, while decorative elements—fruits, grotesques, handles, and lugs—are finally stuck to the piece with slip (liquid clay). Flatware is produced from a mold. The piece of clay is placed in a mold to give it its interior shape, and then pressed against the sides by hand. Hollowware consists of various molded parts assembled and stuck together with slip. All the pieces, including those made by the many students who flock to these potteries to learn the skill, are then dried in the sun. Firing makes the item almost indestructible; it is stable, cannot dissolve, and can last for centuries undamaged.

Clay fired in a 1292°F (700°C) oven takes forty hours to become "biscuit" (its state after the first firing and before glazing); this needs to cool for at least twenty-four hours. Biscuit is strong but porous. Once dried it was dipped in a bath of glaze. The glaze was made of lead oxide, silica to bleach the glaze, and tin. Pottery that is to be decorated is then sent to the painter, who uses cobalt oxide for blue, antimony oxide for yellow, manganese for violet and brown, copper for green, and gold dissolved in acid for the pink color known as "Cassius purple." He or she applies intricate patterns, mythical birds, garlands, birds of paradise, hot-air balloons, or roses. Skill and a steady hand are essential—mistakes cannot be erased!

Jean Faucon of Apt used a very special technique, combining clays, to produce a mixture of shades that resemble the marbled ceramics of Uzès, which use a similar technique. The raw material is used in its natural state: the hills of Rustrel and Gargas contain deposits of a dark red, almost violet earth, veined with brown, green, and even bluish clays.

The Poterie Provençale in Biot still uses the local pink-tinted white clay as the basis for making earthenware pots, glazed mainly in dark yellow, black, and green, as well as for large classic jars.

Each pottery manufactory used to produce its own distinctive style of decoration, developed by the potters and painters. Today many potters buy plain white-glazed pottery and add their own designs, or copy classic decoration. There are three main types of decoration. Firstly there is the "authentic" style, which originated in the seventeenth and eighteenth centuries. It is often

FACING PAGE:
Like lots of studios, the Poterie du Soleil, at Villecroze in the Haut-Var, perpetuates the purity of traditional shapes, such as these water jugs awaiting glazing to make them watertight.

PAGE 186:
The tradition of white faience is very much alive in Varages.

PAGE 187:
The indispensable *tian*, in which summer vegetables are slowly cooked in the oven.

elaborate because noblemen did not want anything that looked too plain or discreet. The "classic" designs came later, and made use of flower patterns, fruits, and garlands. The "contemporary" style allows potters to give free rein to their imagination.

OLD AND MODERN DESIGNS

As soon as the demand for china began, Moustiers outdid Marseilles, Montpellier, and Varages, its rivals. Pierre Clérissy, who by 1679 was known as a "master potter," surrounded himself with painters; within twenty years they had made the village famous. This was the era of decoration known as *à la Berain,* which consisted of hunting scenes and coats of arms taken from collections of the work of Florentine engraver Antonio Tempesta (1555–1630). Birds, flowers, and figures were incised into the glaze. The decoration was consistently blue, but a few touches of ocher would later be added, and eventually it became multicolored. In order to compete with porcelain, earthenware pottery adopted Chinese patterns, then birds and grotesque figures, of the type that can be seen in frescoes in Italian Renaissance villas. The decor was in a single color, usually blue, olive green, or yellow, or sometimes in two colors. There are also mythological decorations surrounded by garlands of flowers known as the "potato-flower pattern," and later "solanum-flower pattern"; this was so popular that it was even copied in China.

French victory at the battle of Fontenoy in 1745 inspired decoration consisting of patriotic flags and trophies; the French Revolution, the establishment of the French Empire, and important scientific discoveries of the period were also recorded by the potters.

In Marseilles, the Spanish were the leading producers of pottery, and the decoration consisted mostly of flower patterns. It was distinctive in that the background glaze was yellow, a sunny ocher, rather than white.

In the 1750s, all the French manufactories produced patterns featuring life-like flowers, Strasbourg producing the best pieces. The Varages flower garlands and the roses painted by the Ferrat brothers at Moustiers were the most popular patterns. In Marseilles, Veuve Perrin's birds and insects depicted in relief were added to the fruits and flowers. Fish and other marine creatures were used in baroque fashion, to decorate a wine-cooler, for example.

DIFFERENT TYPES OF CLAY WITH DIFFERING TONES ARE USED TO MAKE THESE TYPICALLY PROVENÇAL CERAMICS.

However, there are instantly recognizable and never-out-of-fashion classic pieces that continue to be found on contemporary tables. While a cake plate by Veuve Perrin would be a little too elaborate for the modern table, there is nothing more delightful and timeless than the little fruits produced by Sicard of Aubagne, which look like rosebuds or cherries, but are in fact rose hips. Their scarlet color and tiny green leaves stand out against the bright yellow background. Most of the decoration is stamped or sponged on. There is a fairly plain central motif, with a border consisting of a thin garland. This should satisfy those who do not like unpatterned china.

Classic designs that never go out of style include a simple line of colored glaze on the rim of plain or decorated plates and hollowware, and the groove—which may also be edged with beading—that decorated plain china in the seventeenth and eighteenth centuries, especially the octagonal plates of Apt and Dieulefit.

Some potters would not abandon traditional techniques for anything; others create designs in the spirit of the age. The Souleïado stores sell china using *boutis* patterns, such as the Fleur d'Arles.

In Varages, primitive flowers are painted on fine china, and Marcelle and Jeannine Cesana decorate their porcelain with oriental flower patterns. These twin sisters, born at Roubaix in 1930, used to be Limoges porcelain painters, but when the factory closed they moved south to Barjols, near Varages, and have worked for the Manufacture des Lauriers since 1965. The little bowls made by the Poterie Provençale at Biot reproduce Art Deco designs, such as stylized rosettes. The slightly transparent glaze that reveals the pink of the clay, a speciality of Offner at Varages, is particularly attractive.

The Atelier Soleil at Moustiers has developed a glaze, mottled with gray, highlighted by bright pink. Terre et Provence is another special case. This pottery at Dieulefit is extraordinarily popular and its work can be found in stores in many cities. It is tough yet countrified, glazed pottery in traditional shapes, decorated with olives, fruits and flowers, or geometric friezes that are resolutely modern. This is the sort of china that should be used for eating outdoors, an equivalent of the stoneware that is favored in other regions of France.

FACING PAGE:
This shapely piece in mixed clay from Apt dates from the end of the nineteenth century, as evidenced by its surfeit of decoration.

192

LEFT:
A fruit bowl by Pichon in Uzès, distinguishable by the little flowers that embellish the coils.

FACING PAGE:
On Michel and France Loeb's table in their house in the Luberon stands a rare fine-faience wineglass cooler.

PAGES 196–97:
Mottled bowls made from unmixed clay with a multicolor glaze.

FAIENCE IS UBIQUITOUS ON THE TABLE AND IN THE KITCHEN, ITS COLORS HARMONIZING WITH THE REGIONAL CUISINE.

TABLEWARE AND KITCHENWARE

Faience is fairly fragile, unfortunately, and even a slight shock can damage it. It is this disadvantage that has made it less popular than porcelain, which is so much tougher, or glazed terra-cotta, which is more primitive looking but lasts much longer. But faience has other great advantages: the cream color of the paste where it is revealed beneath the glaze and the sensual touch of the piece are incomparable. The edge of the plates are never thin and sharp, as in porcelain, the hollowware is never angular, and the bowls, which fit into the palm of the hand like a morning kiss, are what makes faience pottery so much better than the rest. Just looking at it reveals its superiority: it glitters and glows with reflections that bounce off the grooves in octagonal plates, off the lugs of the soup bowls, and off the knobs and the fruit shapes on the tureen lids.

Factory-made faience is tougher than studio pottery, but it is still elegant due to the clay, the glaze, and the subtle decoration. A more elegant note can be added to the service if the bowls, serving platters, and hors-d'oeuvres dishes are of expensive faience, as these pieces will be subjected to less wear and tear than the other dishes.

"Apartment faience" is the name given to those pieces of china that are displayed between courses, but are never actually eaten from, such as soup tureens, wine coolers, and fruit bowls, of which the finest, arguably, are from Marseilles.

All the hollowware produced by Jean Faucon, whether marbled or not, is of museum quality. Particularly noteworthy are the wonderful covers for vegetable tureens, whose handles consist of a vine branch covered in bunches of grapes, the little marbled cups with a white edge and handle, the woven or pierced baskets in Uzès style, the oil flasks and dessert serving bowls. Candy boxes, pill boxes, and snuff boxes were usually reserved for bedrooms, as were the pitchers and basins used for washing.

One item that should always be made of faience is the *tian*. This is a deep dish, with or without a lid, that is placed in the oven. The tougher and heavier the clay, the tastier the dishes cooked in it. All the summer vegetables—zucchini, eggplant—are cooked in a *tian*, as are meats in sauce that need reheating.

Then come the olive pots and pitchers. The latter are often believed to be purely for keeping water cool, but when they were made of terra-cotta and enameled only on the inside, they were attached in bunches to the neck of

FACING PAGE:
Jean Faucon from Apt works on pieces made from mixed clay from Gargas and Roussillon. This tureen is of fine white faience with a mottled cobalt-blue glaze.

198

FACING PAGE:
The provenance of this dove-gray Louis XVI-style service is discernible by its pearly enamel: it comes from Poët-Laval, near Dieulefit, in the Drôme Provençal.

RIGHT:
A fine faience serving dish with a crackled glaze from Vallauris.

PAGE 202:
A splendid old turned-wood pestle for this marble mortar, which has seen many years of service in the making of *aïoli* and *soupe au pistou*.

PAGE 203:
Cooking utensils, fondue pots, and *tians* are fired at very high temperatures to make them ovenproof. The bowl pierced with holes (bottom, left) was used for washing fruit.

the pedlar's donkey and were used to hold olive oil, which does not like light or heat. There are also jugs, oil-flasks, ovenproof roasting pans, and stewpots made of fireproof pottery, in which civet of hare can simmer over the embers; there are salt boxes and flour boxes, with lids of polished walnut or olive wood, sometimes with spoons. The finest mortars, used to make *aïoli*, *rouille*, and the fragrant paste for *soupe au pistou*, are made from marble, although the more commonly used ones are made from olive wood. Antique examples of the vinegar pot can still be found in Apt faience at the Isle-sur-la-Sorgue, and modern ones in kitchenware stores.

Vallauris is famous for its cookware; roof tiles and bricks have been made there since the eleventh century. When the village was populated by the Genoese in the sixteenth century, kitchenware became the local industry. Feluccas and galleons would stop at Golfe-Juan to load up with pots, pans, and casseroles of every type. They were bound for North Africa, Italy, and Spain. The revival of Vallauris began in the 1920s, when Placide Saltalamacchia, an Italian potter, and his wife opened a kitchen pottery studio that is still going today.

GLASSWARE

There is only one glassmaking center in Provence—Biot. But the village contains so many glassblowers and glassware designers that the classic shapes and colors they use are constantly being enriched with new ideas. The setting is delightful: a hilltop village overlooking pine-covered hills and the noisy gaiety of Antibes. In the studios, visitors can watch the glow of the kilns and the glassblowers as they manipulate the translucent glowing balls of glass. Among the objects produced will be wineglasses, sundae glasses, vases, water pitchers, carafes, and tumblers.

One cannot but enjoy drinking from the stemmed glasses produced in Biot, in which bubbles are imprisoned in a substance that varies in color from bluish-gray, almost white, through cobalt blue. Glassware has many colors in Biot—pink, lavender blue, saffron yellow. True, it is not the ideal wineglass for appreciating the color of a wine, but there are decanters in an almost transparent glass. The hollowware—bowls, vases, and pitchers—is also delightful. An individual piece of Biot glassware stamps the decor as belonging to Provence, and marks its faithfulness to the land.

ACKNOWLEDGMENTS

The publisher would like to thank all those who opened their doors to Christian Sarramon and who made this book possible.

Photographic Credits
All photographs reproduced in this book are by Christian Sarramon, with the exception of the following:
Page 21, top, right and bottom, left: © Isabelle Ducat

Editorial Director: Ghislaine Bavoillot
Design: Isabelle Ducat
Translated from the French by Josephine Bacon, American Pie, London
Editorial Adaptation and Proofreading: Anne McDowall
Typesetting: Gravemaker+Scott
Color Separation: IGS-CP, L'Isle d'Espagnac, France
Printed in Singapore by Tien Wah Press

Simultaneously published in French
as *Maison provençale*
© Flammarion, S.A., Paris, 2014

English-language edition
© Flammarion, S.A., Paris, 2014

PAGES 210–11:
La Danseuse de Farandole, a famous *santon* (a handpainted terra-cotta figurine) from Marseilles, often decorates the mantelpiece in houses in the Arles region.

FACING PAGE:
Baroque satyrs spout fountains of fresh water in the Jardins d'Albertas.

PAGES 214–15:
An old house transformed into a restaurant overlooking the Bassin de Cucuron.